# PRAYER BOOK

# PRAYER BOOK

Matt Mauch

Lowbrow
Press

PRAYER BOOK
Copyright 2011 Matt Mauch

Cover design: Denny Schmickle

Published by Lowbrow Press
www.lowbrowpress.com


ISBN 978-0-9829553-0-7
Second Edition

# CONTENTS*

*Nonfiction annotations for each of the poems in this book can be found on the poet's website (www.mauchmauch.com).*

*invocation*

## Livin' on a prayer

*Half a dryer sheet, not a whole one*
is what I overhear. Is what the young mother
angrily whispers to the young father
as their child sleeps, and doesn't. Sleeps, doesn't.
In a laundromat on a Wednesday afternoon
I pile clean, wet clothes in mounds,
draw warm change from my pocket,
feed the dryer its coins.
If you say it in an empty amphitheater
even if it's an amphitheater
of Maytags
it grows concentrically larger.
The young mother whispers again.
The young father is folding their clothes
*wrong, goddamnit.*
I try to focus on Muzak,
lines I trust to rhyme
that simply aren't there. *Wrong goddamnit*
grows into what I hear:
that the young mother is about to swim. Her stroke
will be the slow, crawling through time stroke
Channel swimmers use.
With my heart's hands
I grease the young mother's body.
I whisper *good luck.*
The young father doesn't know
he's letting down a daughter of Zeus.
He will not be among her handlers
passing food and drink by pole
from a boat. Small, he's made smaller still
by his large mustache. He's trying on
the father coat, washing the hoodlum coat,
stuck in a laundromat
forever, like Sisyphus. I draw the last
of the warm change
from my pocket, feed other coins
into myself. I can't remember the words to a song
I thought I had memorized. Washing
panties, I'm trying to become a better man.

There is a body-mind dualism if I am sweeping the floor
and thinking about Hegel. But if I am sweeping the floor
and thinking about sweeping the floor, I am all one.
Sweeping the floor becomes, then, the most important
thing in the world. Which it is.

– Gary Snyder

## Prayer to be prayed over French fries, green beans, sausages, the rest

Though it's old school
to compare the pods to souls in limbo
I did that, compared them, said fee fi fo fum
under my breath
like a soul-eating giant
with no fairy tale
or myth to inhabit.
Now, I want to knock on the doors
on both sides of the street,
trade what I know
and don't know of the pods
for meals, ad-libbing a role from
the parables my grandparents told
of celebratory times
after a good war.
The pods are dead catalpa pods
that have outlasted winter, have desperately held on
to branches, making the tree (for me)
a monument. By week's end
new pods will be establishing themselves,
pushing out green. The pods that inspire me
will be mowed into mulch,
will degenerate into loam
as the tree grows thick
with heart-shaped leaves. My heart,
less heart-like, is shaped like a stomach.
My stomach beats like a one-valved heart.
My unheralded role in history
begins with collecting pods sufficient
to make a bouquet. Anymore
anytime I eat anything long and thin
I mouth the word survivor.

## Pray that it were otherwise, but the hard work of life isn't in the tapping of the true thought, but in the building of a pipeline to deliver the goods

I have no son, no daughter, but say out loud
*Clean your plate, son. Eat your spuds.*
*Think of your growing muscles,*
*son.* I wait for a *Yes, dad*
to come from the dust
I've never bothered to wipe
from the high shelves. Having heard third-hand
that an old friend's infant daughter
has died, I buy a bouquet of flowers
at a chain store.
Because I buy most of my plants
for a couple bucks each
it's a tribute
to tend to each minute of today
like it's an expensive new tree
from a garden boutique.
The involuntary twitter
in my left cheek, near my good ear,
is seismic, my geology
okaying a volcano burst.
The refrigerator
isn't saying a thing about food. It's droning
a dirge. Is there a better way of saying
*Bill, it's been too long*
than *Bill, it's been too long?*
On the back of papers
a company wants me to fill out
and return, I draw (badly) the underground
parts of a family tree. Without the trunk, etc.,
my doodle looks like a nest.

## A conversation that sounds like me praying
## to the ghost of James Wright
## as if he were here in the passenger seat
## and the things I say might yet become
## an annotation to "A Blessing"


There's only one Indian pony left from the original
two, Jim. Let's tell whomever asks it's
the older one who's gone. Having led the good life
she's buried now and mingling
with a willow's roots. Only
there's no way in hell this pony
behind the fence, three or four miles from Minnesota Lake,
is your pony, is related aside from in the loosest,
evolutionary, begat-from sense.
I've chosen to call this pony *the pony that's left*
because I've come upon it on the road
to Rochester, Minnesota, where each of us ended up
that day my grandfather's sister, my great aunt, the nun,
led me, my smooth hand in hers, to the commissary
at Mayo. I was the blonde-haired boy
reaching to the vats: skim, whole, two percent—
marvelous! My realization that milk
was not simply milk
was the glee you happened upon
in the beverage line, me
less a boy than an arc of light. Jim, it was my thin wrist
that chose the whole. You could finish
your poem. There never was a delicate girl.

## Prayer to that which accepts me in sacrifice

I walk along a shore, look across a lake,
wade in, spread my fingers
so the curvature of my hands
is inverse to the surface of a rock,
honorably seize it, tilt it
up from its bed.
Crawfish that were under it
(and if it's the sleeping head of a god
all my up-the-ladder reincarnations)
turn into silt, clouds
of used-to-be-here. The sun, through heat-haze,
is a gumball
shining through the flesh
of the sky's cheek.
The rock is a rock, the sun
an important star, the best of its light
tinsel on waves.

## Prayer for old fish, hail to their beards
## of monofilament

Lost, I stop to watch a fisherman/woman, can't tell
in a lake I bet
has *big, muddy, lower, green, sandy, duck,* or *bullhead*
in its name, isn't one of the lucky lakes
with an Ojibwe name.
I roll the window down, tell Odysseus
I have no idea what gifts
I owe to the gods of the lovely breeze.
The fisherman/woman is reeling something
reelworthy in, chose the bait
fish couldn't resist, can tell children
that to understand the difference
between a minnow and a leech
sing the song everybody's singing
then try to do the same
with its B side. The logic of 45s
enters the digital age in the suburbs
where I'm late to meet up for lunch
looking for the bar
with the orange moose out front. Sirens
in the not-so-distant distance
don't even attempt
to turn me into meat-of-perch
alive in a body of water less than half an hour ago,
somebody's shore lunch. In the Circe version of my future
I'm eating a corn pancake
with a side of black beans, drinking
a cold Hatuey,
never having found the orange moose
but having convinced myself
Jules, Joseph, Cindy, and Susan
will forgive me
driving back to the city, walking the three blocks
from my place to Victor's, ordering
the usual, texting them this
in installments.

## Crimes of the heart: a prayer to the patron saint of that, on the lam for life

The setting for wishing
you would have done things different
might be the banks of a creek
behind a VFW, on the outskirts of town, at 3 a.m.
on a Tuesday. You don't have, or need, a Marlboro.
You smoke from a fire within.
The moon is full, hanging like a bulb
in an empty warehouse.
You've become your own sentencer.
The creek that would be the soloist
singing the ballad
of the end that forgives the means
is bone smooth, mute.
It's impossible to convince the jury
of dead relatives you answer to
you can make up for things
by sending the emotional equivalent
of some inflation-adjusted cash
in a security envelope
with no return address.
Tonight is a night spent
holding back tears
in the belly of an onion.
Your mind, infused with the liquor of regret,
is the moon that controls the tide
of breathing. Although you haven't
touched it or crawled inside
you've seen one in the library museum
and what you think this feels like
is life in an iron lung.

**Prayer like the punch line that isn't funny**
**to the joke that begins, "So this pagan**
**and this transubstantiator walk into a bar . . ."**


I'm ushered through the dark
by windows and the glow
that comes from inside rooms
lit by butter-yellow pods, rooms
lit by jittery blue, breaching city limits
where uniform rows of soybeans
turn their leaves to the full moon.
In each of the bean pods
deities in the fetal position
demand, from light,
more of these 24-hour shifts.
Standing among them
is like wearing
star-toed shoes.
My arching brow's
a high window from behind which
a featureless face looks down.
The upturning of the open-mouthed head
is square-peg me
rearranging how I fit
into the body's round hole.
I feel like a whale in air,
like I leapt and got stuck.
I unshell a handful of beans.
Each one of them's too hard to chew.

## The invisible burden I carry:
## a prayer to appease the god of gravity
## who has gathered these seven moons
## in elliptical orbits around me

I love how my old silver pen is dented where its held
in the teeth, grooved where the fingers have worn
sickle paths, as if the metal were as amenable to marking
as is the wood of my favorite chopsticks.
The pen's molten blue tail
is like a comet's, longest when hope carries the day,
when it feels as if each pore has opened
to let the light in, and light, necessarily,
does the job it has to do,
shrinks the exiled soul
to a speck, and the silver pen says
*In imitation of a poppy seed*
*that weighs as much as a city.*


•


Say I'm body, you're soul,
wed now

do you love me or love to hate me
for my tendency not to go there
unless I can do so on foot?

for the dangerous way I walk,
head down, running into sign posts,
bruising skin?

for studying toes as
they hit their heads on the ceiling
of shoes?

for the tongue that tells you
they're burial mounds leading the way?

•

At a wide open window, the outside
comes in. Welcome to the congregation
of the beautiful spring day. Remove your shirt.
Does the body, a disbeliever, sag?


•


If one were lured by the peppers
growing like suns in pots
on the ledge, and if next one mistook,
in slanting sun, the open window and lack of glass
for perfectly clear glass, and
if furthermore one leaned in to flatten
a cheek or nose against the cool perfection,
one would fall to one's death.


•


This afternoon, under the clouds
that will bring the rain we need, I'll drink
the sun tea brewing now in a jar
leeward of the temptress peppers, like
a species forgotten, the small print
none of us bother to read.


•


The jar is both dormant, and dominant,
in my view. The blades of grass beyond it
wave like the fingers of baleen
you'll find in a whale's mouth.
I go outside, deep within the belly
of the day, more like a dime passing through
than a grape.

•

If an informant told you
this is the place
where the transparent and the opaque
were hammering out a deal,
and if you turned the door handle
slowly, sneaked in, what
you'd find is me saddling
the window ledge, a dissatisfied picture
trying to leak out of its frame.

## Psalm of the small-town street dance

This noon, as every noon,
the steeple bells of eight denominations
ring all at once. We listen like three thousand bugs
caught in a jar. The questions we almost ask
are kept in check by cops
who have parked their cars
and mounted horses. The handbills
are printed and hung like a caption beneath us.
Blowhole or no, it says
*swims*. The marching band's accompaniment
tumbles from anthem to cadence
to echo of a ditty we can't get out of our heads.
We use our coins and cash
like slings and rocks, lean into each other
like window shoppers
in the tractor beam of the first TV,
refuse to admit we know each other
no better than we know the river
when we swim deep, can't see through silt,
bump into the adapted blind,
get bit. We squeeze into costumes.
Those among us who are limestone
soft offer up the body for carving,
allow initial after initial inside
heart after heart to reduce
the self to sand. O Goliath donning
the gaudy scarves of sunset, the wig
of twilight, coming in drag,
we aren't the alloy we want to be
just yet.

## A prayer for student success not wrongly misconstrued as another conversation with the ghost of James Wright, presuming that, after body-death, you believe he appears in my office to help me grade

Jim, did you teach the wrists
as much as you taught the minds?
Yesterday I had to ask, *Where was I?* having lost focus
watching a wrist keep its place in a book. It wrote
elegant cursive in the same
way it slaughters hogs, gathers
the least obviously usable parts,
stuffs them into blue metal cans,
the cans into cardboard boxes
upon which a machine has stamped
SPAM. Before class and their shifts
they meet up in pickup trucks
in the main student lot, all the engines
running, Jim, because April still feels like
winter, so the windows steam,
and some print in block letters,
and I see Zapruder-esque films
of their quickies on the bench seats
after bag lunch, the parking lot outside the window
seen through the lens of my dollar-store heart
hosts orgies wherein wrists
make their way like worms
into and through clothes,
books, body . . . writhing, Jim,
not fruitlessly, but as the worm scientist
would say *fragmentationally*. Doing it
just because.

## How Operation Desert Storm reminded me poem is prayer

The morning after the war began
I picked my *Complete Pocket Walt Whitman Anthology*
up from the floor, rescuing it
from beneath the night stand, where it was face down,
open, recovering, like me, from drink.
I blew dust off the book's spine. Walter
being Walter, I feared the words had gone wild,
were leaking through the floorboards, rafters,
into the apartment below.
Via life-after-death-mouth-to-mouth
Walter mother bird fed my abode
a meal of "I Sing the Body Electric."
I turned to the "Drum Taps" section
and sitting on the toilet shined
my made-of-air carbine, packed neat rows of clips
in imaginary ammo boxes, fell in love
with my own voice repeating
nothing new. Next
voice I fell in love with
arrived at work, via telephone, belonging
to Allison from Orion Pictures, Inc.,
who called seeking weekly grosses
for Depardieu's *Cyrano*.
I took my cue from Walter's deep vision,
told Allison I could see
miles of open front between us,
blue, pink, and yellow states,
fortified black borders,
town names too tiny to read,
capitals and county seats
marked by stars. Allison said that she could see
the borderless topographical map. She spent
a full minute describing marble cake
cooling on her kitchen counter,
chocolate frosting
lying in wait. We played paper-scissors-rock
on absolute faith. I answered her question:

five thousand sixty-three dollars, no cents.
I hung up the phone
and in a song to myself promised
if I ever have a kid I'll name it Allison
or Alvin or Ali or Al,
that my next dog (or cat) will learn to come,
heel, sit, roll over, play dead, and fetch
to either Walter, Wally, or Miss Whitman.

## We pray to the lord: lord hear our prayer (omerta)

For former San Jose Police Chief Joseph McNamara, who said, *A corrupt, racist or brutal cop will abstain from misconduct only when he looks at the cop next to him and believes that the officer will blow the whistle if he hits the suspect.* For officer McNamara, we pray:

> The last time I put a shell to my ear, the Ocean
> (I pissed in sand instead of in it) admitted
>
> its consent to becoming a poster child
> for Sweetness & Light
> was given under the duress
> of Mother Nature's extortion.

For the anonymous San Francisco cop who said, *When a command staff has a tendency to overlook the internal infractions or downplay them, they (the younger officers) see that as support for 'the working cop,' as protecting the integrity of the organization.* For anonymous cops, we pray:

> I put out food for cardinals,
> goldfinches, chickadees, orioles, jays
>
> and
> with the same hands
> on the same day
>
> pump up a pellet gun,
> shoot at pigeons, sparrows, squirrels.

For the second anonymous San Francisco cop who said, *The brass doesn't seem to get how disdainful our community already is of their police, how they see us as a necessary evil. You can't go to a community meeting and not feel that venom that so many of these people have against us, that total disdain.* For communities, we pray:

> At a café downtown, people eat alone, across
> from empty chairs,

no candlelight, no flowers, if

they were birds
with eyes where their ears
are they'd stare at each other
instead of down

at fork, knife, spoon
wrapped with a napkin
sealed with a cuff
of orange paper.

**Prayer that I will be reborn next as one
of the tiny living things for whom the universe
is a drop of rain, its Big Bang being
the snow temperature moment
between cold water and ice**

1. The soft and violent *thrrth thrrth*, i.e., an orange rind tearing.
2. The lubricated gear-grind, terra firma rumble, also called: buses, passing.
3. The *pank-ity-pank, thooth-fwop*: mail through the mail slot door.

These are ordnance aimed at embryonic thoughts.
I set my cheeks upon pedestal hands, am forlorn
in its *wandering forlorn of Paris once her playmate*
sense, like a man in a homburg
walking with my head down, stuck in one of the shapes
our bodies assumed in the 1930s,
when dust was blamed for the malaise.
Photos at the library capture us
before we learned about our manufacturer's
planned obsolescence. You can find them
in dark aisles where light enters
only from the side, where a spleen would be
if a heart were there to feed it, if
the building were a body. Yesterday I stole
a photo with a caption that said, *The Deepest
Winter Ever.* In it, an unidentified man, his hat
and long coat covering like a tarp
has just passed the barber shop, eyes down,
so forlornly you could say
forlorn is a sport, that the man's in a zone
looking earthward at his shoes
awed by them spending their lives
molding themselves to the bottoms of his feet,
sizing himself up to about a hundred dollars
in leather, stitching, style.

## A trapper knows three prayers

*For preparation*
    I turn the flashlight down,
    can almost see
    by the blue light
    of the brightening sky. Wind
    announces wind,
    fish detonate cover bombs of silt
    flee upstream
    through the creek's claim in the land,
    water on pilgrimage, chaste enough
    to eradicate murk.

*For killing*
    Swing for the sweet spot
    between coal-black eyes. The swung-at
    thrashes and dives.
    Swing, thrash, dive, surface, repeat. Poke
    at the carcass, spin its belly to the sky,
    release a scarlet wisp of blood
    that rings you
    like Saturn.

*For thanks*
    I drag the beaver to the car, consider the view from above,
    blaze a nonsensical configuration
    in my farmer-friend's field, roll
    the window down,
    switch the heater to high, drive stocking-footed
    back to and through a town just
    beginning to stir. Rising from all the houses:
    columns of steam in the shapes of bodies,
    full and partial nudes, beasts,
    children,
    the armless accepting the fact of armlessness,
    Venus de Milo
    buried beneath us, dreaming
    of that which she was made in the image of.

## Psalm for the working class in a totalitarian regime doing double duty as a prayer for the same class opiated by dreams of wealth in a capitalistic one

I didn't notice until now—right now—
9:28 a.m., Monday, September 3,
that the radio I keep in the kitchen
has been on for days, the volume so low
I have to bend down to hear, have to kneel,
listen out, around. Who *would* have heard it,
this white noise & buzz, with all the mowers
throwing their voices, echoes
of knives buttering toast? Eating
the last of the pasta and sauce
I made three days ago, I remember tuning
the radio delicately, positioning the needle
on a singer-songwriter station, singing along
to "Volare," belting out sounds
when I didn't know the words. On behalf
of the deejay who took a break during a longish song,
wandered among grasses out back,
caught them in a yawn, believed
he was inside a mouth, I sing "Volare"
again, strain against the idea of *a cappella*
as if *a cappella* were black water
and I was falling in. The deejay
turned, sort of ran, found himself at center
no matter where he turned or ran.
I take my boots off, rub my ugly, calloused feet
until they feel like they've been cut
from marble slabs, and honed.

## The human palimpsest's prayer

I want to stop being so human,
low to the ground, dragging this
bag of bones around, udder with nothing
left to give, no memory of grip pull twist squeeze,
how it lets the inside out. I want to stop
making my way through the day
like I'm a shim. Want to forget about the mallet
driving the shim, climb the highest tree in town,
settle on a branch that can barely hold me,
encouraging the slenderer branches
higher up: *Prick the firmament,*
*bleed down a sample of beyond.*
I want to leave the cellar I've packed full
behind me, squinting as I would to see someone
coming toward me from faraway, blurring
the orange and yellow leaves, the few trees still green,
softening the world, merging the seldom merged,
valley and city and river reclining
like paint-spackled nudes.
I want to channel the Gustav Klimt
Gustav Klimt always wanted to be,
to turn osprey, owl, or crow, marveling
at the surprising ease of flight, joints
cracking in places where I never imagined
I could bend.

## The moon tonight inspires not only wonder and tides but also this deathbedish prayer

It lands on and blocks the road in front of me, more
Jupiter than moon. I look
left, right: I'm in a room
wallpapered with cottonwoods. The moon is rolling a carpet out,
it's made of pregnant light . . . I call it that, driving
into it I say *the pregnant light*
*is bleaching the trees.*
I leave the car door open, key in the ignition. The finders
of abandoned things will think, *What happened*
*happened quick. This was an emergency.*
I kill a mosquito, and as instinctively
as I do so am sorry for what I've done,
that I am shadow, man, can't
dismantle the border between.
I breathe in whatever the night
exhales. It's like I'm making out
with lilacs and moon.
I sit with my back against a tire,
get on the hood,
absorb the engine's heat
until I feel like the one solid thing
at the heart of a nebula.
I get down from the hood clumsily, forget
I inhabit a mass others can see,
put my head back, settle into the contours
of the ditch. Waiting would be different
if I had never read that the pull
of the right kind of body
in the right conditions, given time, is enough
to draw everything to a center.
It would be different, I'm telling you, if the moon
were saying anything other than *take*
*an inventory, invent a tool.*

## Prayer for the specialists who sooner or later will be tasked with fixing me

Trying to cross Hennepin Avenue at night
when it's varnished with rain
is dyed by lights
of clubs and 24-hour commerce
so that it looks like an Oriental rug, like the chicken
who's just been told the joke
about the chicken crossing the road
and doesn't get it
I stop in the middle of the street
wonder what tricks
a surgeon fixing the body
uses, if a patch
is worn over the eye that sees
the luminescence inside, so a vision
of staple and stitch, a shaved sternum—the distance
of an imagined end a few hours from now
is the thing that allows hand and scalpel
to impose order at the heart,
a heart that, when you're close in,
and it's dying, must transfix
like a blossom unfolding in a time-lapse film,
must be as hypnotic as car horns and city noise
converging to make song
like they're following a score
you swear they've spent
yours and your parents'
and grandparents' lives
rehearsing. In the middle of the street,
heart of the city, incandescents
& fluorescents whisper, neons shout.
*Can you remember where it was*
*you were in such a hurry to get to?*

## Prayer for my oldest teachers

I walk beneath an elm that didn't catch Dutch elm disease,
elm I should learn from, elm the crow
that calls the shots
dubbed *the* tree, announcing, *This*
*fits our number, is our roost.*
I walk across the litter of crows
splattered on the sidewalk
like a bridge of stars. I'm not shat on
because I'm diplomatic enough
to start the day unarmed.
The first crows leave with a single caw each
five crows on repeat
telling me I should swim
in the sky like it's a sea, that paths will be revealed
are being revealed
right now. The crows have convinced me that one's
movement through it, the reaching out and cupping
of a handful, the strong return, the twist,
the lift and reaching again—
if yours is as slow as a manta ray's stroke, you won't
need water to swim in
yet swim is exactly
what you'll do. The crows
are saying those who own rope
and grappling hooks
who are willing to throw them
will also have to decide if they're ready
to climb. At night I listen
for heads being tucked under wings,
mouths breathing though feather masks.
It should be easiest to keep track
of the business of crows
after it snows. It snows. What's easy to see
is that the air rights of crows supercede
those of the city. The elm's
a bouquet of wire. The crows are leaving it
one by one. If I'm translating crow correctly
what this means

is there will be times
when we'll need to give each other
at least a quarter of a mile of elbowroom
and not being crow we'll need to do it
like contortionists, within the confines of a patio
or bedroom, or what's even more likely
is everyone will gather in the kitchen
and it's there that we sardines
will have to pretend we're whales.

## Prayer for ferrying

The lawn crew my neighbor has employed
puts the equivalent of a cherry atop the sundae
of their work: a sign that says
for 48 hours kids and dogs
shouldn't play here. I cross the property line,
hold out my palm, a cracked plot of hand
like soil damaged by draught
that, today, is a bridge I extend
to a death-sentenced milkweed plant. A caterpillar
like a Nagasaki survivor
crawls from the underside of a leaf
onto my hand, goes back and forth
from hand to hand. It and I
are naked seeking the shade
of window boxes, ledges, handrails,
mailboxes, shelves
where we can be cocooned
or chrysalised for a very long time
unaware that moon works on behalf
of sun, that the business sun and Round Up
are in is repossessing
hiding places. DISCLAIMER RE: WISHES
COME TRUE: those who emerge
as monarch butterflies
live a life like pleasure boating
in a yacht with a full-time crew.
Most come out day moths.
For them each day is an ocean crossing.
What they're crossing it in: a duck-hunter's skiff.

## Prayer to bestow a blessing on the city

The Neanderthals wrote their histories in soft wood,
passed along their cosmologies in gestures. Me
I'm trying to do something as ephemeral as that
for the inventor of the red light, for the genius conceiver
of the DON'T WALK sign, for the time they've given
me to figure out that *city* rightly considered
is a contraction of *gravity*, code for the inward pull
of humans in binary pairs. It's black-holish
this falling in on myself, wondering
if after death we're allowed to crowd
the one-consciousness kiln, to mob the gates
or if we must go in an orderly fashion, one
at a time, buck-naked, no assurance
lovers will and enemies won't
be fused together. After an overpriced
but expense-able lunch alone, on the streets
of a downtown unstrange in its echo of the Platonic
form for town square, peculiar, though, in its execution—
too many pharmacies, no tobacconists—
no longer wearing the mask I wear for business,
one blonde stone set among the darker rest
at the top center of a building
overshadows me. The builder, rather than leaving his name,
as was fashionable, etched only 1883
into its face. I cross the street, address a partly cloudy sky
with only my eyes, ask how many of us, once all that's left
of us is a body, must be melded together
to make a brick? My toes in my shoes
in my socks, shackled and enslaved
sadly attempt the midair pose
made famous by cliff divers on postcards.
Take a countenance and remove its skull,
you have a building façade. Next to the revolving
door's hydra of bullet-proof tongues, face to face
with a building ready to eat me, I kiss a brick
warmed by sun, just to taste it.

Only one sweeter end can readily be recalled—
the delicious death of an Ohio honey-hunter,
who seeking honey in the crotch of a hollow tree,
found such exceeding store of it, that leaning
too far over, it sucked him in, so that he died
embalmed.

– Herman Melville

**Black wool as the answer to everything,**
**the antidote for, the synonym of,**
**in medias res, black wool is love—**


There's an itch across my back.

> Black wool follicles
> grow conjoined though glad pores,

blanket of wool cocooning
me as I croon: O

> there's not enough praise for wool,
> black wool.

I can't bring myself to scratch the itch.

> An enormous ebony spider
> has spun and is spinning
> the universe.

The Milky Way's stuck
like a bug.

> Are you lounging
> in your dreams
> in pasture with your arms
> around the shoulders

> > of the getting naked-er
> > as we get hairy-er
> > > donor sheep?

Wrap your eight legs
around me. We'll sleep, like the jailed,
> on sheets of wool, sleeping the sleep
> of black wool sheep

> > like dead pharaohs
> > or worms tunneling through

dead pharaohs.

How chosen-one
to give up
this for that, to embrace

a worm's or dead pharaoh's
caste, rejecting wine, song, knives, spoons,
trumpets, bunting, guilt—

                sleeping eternal black wool sleep—

no infernos, beatitudes, treasures,
boots, alarms, or rain

to wake us up. I kiss black wool,
                    turn it to trousers,
                    flames, leaves, spin
                    ruby-black wool

         into black wool I—

                at ten below zero, a halo of wool
      protects my brain
                from frostbite.

I shovel an eight-inch snow
from woolen steps. It's like shoveling
eight inches of dead skin
after an eight-day angel orgy.

                To become woolen
                is to emerge from underground
                caked in earth.

Hatched from wool
        is a bird who hears things

at the decibel level of melting snow. It flaps
its wings so fast it seems wingless, beak tearing into

                what's next.

A black and woolen rope
        drops from what you might call

            up there.

I reach for it. A dog that wants it as much as me
growls at black wool I,

a gray and yellow-haired dog
raised on scraps of wool

            dragging its shadow
            and in the shadow, which is seething:

            the steam engine,
            the wheel,
            the formula for maintaining orbit.

This shaggy-haired and stray olive dog
carries the repentant morning sun

            on its mutt-gray back.

Hold velvety black prismatic hologram wool
to the light

        and turn it, redirect
        the light to the street

        where traffic stops
        for what has the feel
        of an accident:

            a black woolen wrecker
            police cars

and flashing emergency lights. Waiting for word,
everyone's tapping woolen feet.

        A black blues ditty
        is played at the speed of

barbed-wire
blood-black
wool.

The dead make a stew
with steel, glass, and plastic
as the broth.

From the bowl of the night,
with my hologram fingers,

I eat the stew
using an every-drop spoon.

Who robbed the cricket of hair?
Hey, cricket, take some of mine.

The spider has hair. There's
the hairy fly. There's partaking
of hairy me.

Cricket must have hairs
I can't see with a woolen lens.

What I can see: the almost-clogged heart
in a creek-bed pebble,

trout
using their hands
spinning a black wool tunic.

They could raise a barn
if they wanted

these trout

dancing an underwater
half out of water
dance,

a black wool ballet.

It's raining wool, black wool. Woolly cricket,
make a C note with your one leg awkward
against mine.

      A globule of hail
      falls past my window, collides with pavement,

      makes twelve less-significant globules of hail

      that dance like mad scientists

      racing to invent a black wool umbrella.

Tomorrow, wet or white, at eight o'clock a.m.,
drinking black wool coffee in my kitchen,
steam and nose hair mingling,

           I'll belch black wool
           out an open window

                      winning the race.

My two X's lose to your three O's
is sad

      but not the saddest song
      you're likely to hear tonight.

The one dream I analyzed according to the dream book
       ,   led me to believe
             I was eating my own tail,

was a black-wool dervish
boiling over in snow-cover'd fields,

trying to survive winter
where winter feels like
tuberculosis.

      A cloud fills up.

Pavement cracked by roots
is also stained by leaves,

is clearly an enemy
of trees.

My footprints in snow
        expose the snow's Achilles heel.

I am both
the slow water beneath the frozen river
                and the man rolling bread into balls
        to use as bait for carp.

                                Fix me a drink, a stiff one.

Touch lightly the crack through which neon
has seeped, and you're touching

        me, saboteur of signs.

                        If a cat's claw you must be
                be a cat's claw
                on the road to clawlessness,

pulling carpet in spite.

        Dear echo of bells: talk with me
        who am what seems like inadequate root structure
                        for a heavy trunk.

                Despite me, the tree thrives.

Sea foam bogards the beach.

What needle doesn't weep for a pulled out stitch?

It's brave beyond brave,
the lamp not plugged into a wall.

                I sold what was stamped SOUL

to the Johnny Appleseed of bridges,

our transaction taking place
in the pungent air
above the imprint of a hoof
in mud.

The pupil of steam's
dilated.

Coins in the pockets
of the just-dead
are warm, almost hot.

The leak in a forest ceiling is responsible
for the balance of hawks,
                        the graffiti of wind.

I bend to the gospel of apes,
cross the country on the exoskeletons of pioneer hope,
crest hill after hill.

O black woolen fingers,
pollinate!

    Star light, star bright, star of black wool night:
    I almost passed out in the shower.
    I spat out what tasted like the bad, settled on my knees.
    The distance from my lips to the showerhead
    was insurmountable.

What was I thinking, thinking
I could breathe through my hands?

On a floor that feels like the ocean
floor I have what feels like a blow hole.

    I crouch and kick
    from three, from
            seven miles deep,

burst through knitted waves
over sailing boats

trailing sea goo,
smudged with woolen residue,
                    cell under a microscope

          with a bunch of other cells
          and we all seem
          selfish.

Come with a torch, then switch
          to a lit match

          when you get really close.

Whatcha gonna do about
                    the bribe in my eyes?

Leopards break into the temple and drink to the dregs
what is in the sacrificial pitchers; this is repeated
over and over again; finally it can be calculated
in advance, and it becomes a part of the ceremony.

– Franz Kafka

## 22nd floor to lobby: transcript of an impromptu prayer

Because there are mirrors,
because of the Cold War and James Bond,
I presume there are cameras watching. Pressing
STOP will satisfy my longing
to find out if paramedics or cops
are quickest. No signal on my cell. I tip my glass
less these days to the good health of those
who've disappeared without a trace, more to the ones
making a go of it without them. In the LED version
of the numeral 16, I see a skunk,
the dog who took the brunt of its spray,
an acquiescent spaniel
who let me wash her in tomato juice
twice a day for nearly a week.
I've stopped reading news
of the skunk-like and spanielesque
due to nightmares centered around
my task to procure the depths
of tomato juice we need.
Being consoled is different than being forgiven.
Neither involves a screen.
Like a bird with a glitch in my calculus
I'm crashing into the same window
again and again, hitting it
until my brain is too numb
to signal my wings.
The corpse I'll make is in many ways as big
as an elephant's. It's going to be the hard work of others
that digs the grave I fit.
Elephant: biggest casket, deepest
cemetery hole you've ever seen. Elephant:
might never rot all the way through.

## Prayer for those flying solo on jet planes ascending and descending through turbulence reminded of the ghost on a bicycle ghost-riding stairs

The girl across the aisle, with the window seat,
says she's going to dream of Chicago, pops
Dramamine, pulls her hood over her face,
becomes a gull hovering near a pier in an imaginary
windy city. Rothko said
we should stand as close
as our nose allows. I toss
toward the girl-gull's beak my
hope that near-death experiences shrink
to pinpricks like headlights
from a slow car passed miles ago.
The girl-gull cups her wings,
looks like an eyelash
under a microscope. She takes
bread from my palm. She's
a god pruning the universe,
swallowing bad-fruit stars
too dim to fire-up life
on planets whose oceans, air, and cupboards
contain the ingredients for it. She eats the bread version
of me as a rock hiding a sun within. The bread
runs out. I become the gull on the piling next to the girl,
tell her it's my turn to warm the eggs.

## Drinking feels like praying when done across the street from a beach where emergency response crews have been conducting a search for over an hour

Janice, she says her name is, hypothesizes
a wormhole big enough to drive a truck through
opens whenever a person dies
from drowning.
Prove it just a little bit, I tell her,
or convince me you can, given money and time,
and I'll figure out a way to communicate
from beyond, will be the suicide who tests the theory, you can watch
me wade in *deep* deep
taking the same sort of pleasure
Stephen W. Hawking must take
in being too brilliant
for the body,
letting my weakness weigh me down,
sucking in water with it, sinking
until I'm nothing
but light dispersed.

## Prayer to encourage the seizing of the day

Because the world didn't end
when the century turned, as my Baptist friend said it would,
I find a seat, become one of the well-packaged humans
on the free bus, wait to depart
from one of the State Fair's park -n- ride lots.
I tell the woman next to me, who has taken her heels off,
replaced them with sneakers and ankle socks,
locked her valuables in the trunk
that I heard, on the radio, on the way over
the lead singer of a band I saw in a bar once
has killed herself for no good reason.
I say, "It's the same reason every time."
Over the P.A. loudspeaker, employee #340542B,
or C, cuts in on a song, tells us
remember to hydrate and wear a hat,
report the unusual, the out-of-place. Blind trust
is what we give an underpaid driver to usher us
to a few square miles of public land, where all signs
indicate that neither the woman with the afternoon off
nor I, not having told each other our names,
will be coming away with a story of how we met
on the bus the year the bridge fell.
We've become experts at resisting the temptation
to remove our street clothes, to leap from building to building
in a single bound, clutching, instead,
the simpler truth of an armrest,
the fact that all we'll be today are bodies fattening up
for winter, mind sacs with a looped
reel repeating: *cheese curds, corn dogs, pronto pups—*
*Scotch eggs, mini donuts, troutwurst—Oh*
*beautiful for spacious skies, land that I love,*
*save room for onion fritters, for*
*pork chops on a stick.*

## Walking is a kind of prayer when done on new snow after midnight

Like a television signal
sullying the air, I stamp my boot-maker's logo
into the wet white. This
is what the first sea creature to brave the land
wished its brain were big enough
to do: study how the heel
lands, the odd way some of us
dig in with the outsides of our feet.
The orange dome of the city, aka
the residual glow of gathering,
lights the sidewalk
like this was pre-ordained, me
walking around the block to see how I've gotten
to where I am, lapping myself in the race
that isn't a race
is me against me. On evergreen
limbs, lightly settling on boughs
all around and above, the shavings of snow
become a snow, the white weight accumulates
like peoples on the plates of the earth.

## Prayer disguised as an open letter to the impatient young man standing with me in line

You almost lost your temper
when a gentleman, not your father,
put his arm on your shoulder,
called you "Son." I'm writing to say
don't give yourself away like that. Don't ask,
as you did, whether you can reach
down from hood-level to change the filter
or if you need to rent some time on a hydraulic hoist
to come up from underneath. What you've got to understand
about this world is doing your own work
voids the warranty. Here's the skinny, kid:
We are in and are responsible
for, at minimum, some two dozen lines all at once.
Like the night clerk in the old Dayton's ramp
it's easier to learn the words that
defer, to smile, nod, ask
how you can help. Is it okay if I call you
Grasshopper? Grasshopper,
there's this T-shirt people used to wear
when waiting in line was like a washed up comic—
like an old Bob Hope in that it couldn't find
the people's pulse. On the shirt
a cartoon eagle is about to grab
a cartoon mouse. The mouse is flipping off
the eagle. "The Last Act of Defiance"
is the caption. Grasshopper, who do you think
told the mouse that now *right now*
is the time to tell the eagle
what the eagle doesn't care to be told
ever? A voice from inside?
Inside you is a widow watching TV
waiting to see the commercial again
so she can write the number down.
She knows you want to dig a hole
where the deed says you can't, that you'll unsheathe
a machete, threaten to split the baby in two.
This widow's wearing the T-shirt.

She wants you to get into that mouse's
head. She sees a future in which you act
like the sun, teaching green to a leaf.
Widow says carry a pencil and a pad. Figure out
what a fella does when he doesn't suspect
he's being tailed. Don't go anywhere ever
again without your pencil, your pad.
Write things down
on the widow's behalf.

## Shopping during the afternoon rush, not buying items on my list if the artery in which the thing is found is clogged with humanity, composing as I nod hello this prayer for intestinal fortitude

Sooner rather than later I'll regret
not committing myself to the time it takes
to procure a jar of pickled beets
in an aisle tight with people, carts.
In a grocery store
when experts say I should be,
my stomach full, here
though
when the rest of the world shops
after setting my alarm last night
to prevent this, meaning
I'd make a weak white blood cell,
would be on the wrong side of the ledger
in the blood you want, blood you don't
accounting. In that apple-sized snowball
grows Astrodome-huge
on its way down the mountain
sense, people everywhere are standing
as if posing for stills
of the next Dachau
or Bergen-Belsen. Explaining
me in the vernacular, your doctor would say
*Depend on him, you'll die.*
I pick out a sack of oranges.
I own an appliance
that turns them to juice.

## Waiting for fireworks: an Independence Day prayer

This backyard is Everybackyard, I am Everyman,
moving part in a one-day exhibit
in the natural history of the lawn chair,
officially observed
bank holiday. I fix a drink,
lose track of the conversation
in a circle of acquaintances and friends
unanimous in their public derision, their private longing
for hot dogs & potato chips. A bruise-colored pigeon
on a second story window AC
coos. I try to understand it,
cocked-head gathering in
sound through my good ear
same way I'd try to make sense of a question
asked by a pleasant stranger
in broken English. I've nothing to add
to a conversation veered
to interior decorating. I go in and out,
translating pigeon, speaking English.
Photos are passed around
of a summer home for sale in Florida. I do
as the pigeon suggests: tap the VACANCY sign
on the hotel next door to the house, trace the features,
show Margaret a neon face. The mothers
go in to breastfeed. The never-have-been-mothers
join them. The screen door slamming
scares off my pigeon. The new-and-never-have-been-
fathers, we refresh our GTs, try to coin new slang
for vagina, something to replace twat,
snatch. Swirling ice in our drinks,
staring at limes, we realize that the pigeon
was Everypigeon, each of us was listening,
each of us now is lost.

## Once upon a time: a prayer for abandoned beginnings

*I think this is very nice, how you get up on the back of*
*time and ride and you don't know where it will go or how*
*it will try to throw you off.*

—Miss Noi

If I measure it, count it out *bip-bap* it really was a long, long *bap* time ago, and it probably should, but does not *bip* seem like a galaxy *bip-bap* far, far away *bip* how could it when it still makes me mad *bap* although I don't mean angry-mad *bip-bap* or swear an oath of revenge *bap* mad, or take twenty paces, turn and fire *bip-bap* forget to feed the kids *bip* mad, my fingers pinching things that aren't there *bap* mad, no, mad here means it ticks *bip-bap* inside of me like water dripping *bip-bap* from a faucet in a sink, it being something *bip-bap* if remembered in other quarters *bip* is probably remembered differently *bap* if, as I said, it's remembered at all, for of the many *bip-bap* seeds we have the opportunity to be either water or sun to *bip* nobody knows *bip-bap* which will be the one *bap* to mutate well, get it right, grow the cure for everything *bip* in its bark, in a paste made from its leaves *bap* although having lived long enough to see better ends *bip-bap* emerge from sketchier starts, my madness *bip* builds an access road *bap* to my sadness, and by that I don't mean *bip-bap* here's a shovelful of dirt for your grave *bap* sad, don't mean *bip* can you imagine 10,000 people dead just like that *bip-bap* sad, no, what I mean is *bip* I have a story I will never be able to tell you *bap* about a town, a house, a road *bip-bap* that's the kind of sad I mean *bip* sadness with no middle or end *bap* complicated by my fear that one day a curator of memory *bap* an agent of me, for my own *bip-bap* good will dampen the drip using not only the brain's, or a brain's, but my brain's approximation of a wash rag *bap* folded and set *bip-bap* beneath the spigot.

## Prayer inscribing a book of pressed leaves

If it works for you, the light
the dead brought back to life
say they see, symbol of things immortal, sit
with me in a parked car on a gravel
road where I've pulled off
the highway's asphalt
and the light does not seem
to be as carefree as
it ought to be, tiring itself out
like an obedient dog
obeying, pillars of it
shining through holes in
cumulonimbus clouds, like
fingers kneading leaves
fallen to the ground
in a grove of trees, where I'm as fascinated
as I used to be when I studied
my grandmother's fingers
making crust from scratch,
pressing it into a pie tin.
The leaves in the light
are chartreuse, a yellow like
a rubber fishing lure, color
of the belief that after weaning
you can return to suckle.

## Prayer to be mumbled softly between flights over a bloody mary in the airport bar

Take just those I call
my close friends, if they had brushes
and paint and talent and painted
me after my death, I would be unrecognizable
from gallery to gallery, frame to frame.
If my enemies and ex
thises and thats
could paint and had painted me
their depictions would be grotesques.
In the self portrait the fear, not of flying,
but of not-flying once you're airborne
paints—a diptych on the back of eyelids—
I'm a bulb in a light fixture
in a rented kitchen,
mounted to the ceiling, restrained by cord,
moonish
over meals and drinks
and card games, mesmerized
by betting and bluffs,
the hands that everyone hides.

**From a parking lot, in an unfamiliar part of town,
eating take-out sushi, listening to talk radio
during a midday break, day of mandatory training,
comes this prayer of gratitude for all of the above**

If only it were as easy
to abandon my worldly pursuits
as it is to kill the engine
in my Jeep.
I close my eyes, picture my alveoli
incessantly toiling,
am like a physicist
at the precipice of theory, tracing
my breathing to the reach of its roots.
It's like following a loon
that sinks beneath the surface,
finding underwater
that my father anchors each breath,
my alveoli wear his face.
I breathe out.
I steam the glass.
I wipe the glass
with the soft part of my fist.
I breathe on the glass again.

## Psalm of the line from a song you can't get out of your head

Before Lou Reed was
Lou Reed in my rearview mirror
he was the man who stood out. I saw him
from what would be considered
a bad camera angle
in the aisle where I couldn't find
my cheese, where all I could make out
was male, dressed head to toe in black.
Now I see sunglasses, curly hair,
the signature thin line
of an upper lip, and I wonder most
not why he's in St. Paul
but why he's chauffeurless,
is driving a Chevy. In
my bag I have bread, juice, bananas,
tomatoes, fish, and rice,
which isn't close to being everything
I need. I have taken advantage
of an end-of-summer sale on locally grown,
over-ripe cantaloupes.
I turn left, watch Lou Reed
turning right. What I won't
do next is go out and buy
his records at the used stores, becoming a fan
simply because of this. Tonight, though,
when I eat my melon I'll
wield a spoon like it's the key that
unlocks me, waiting as long as it takes
for the melon to reveal whether
I'm organic or android, eating, singing
*And the colored girls go do,*
*do-do, do-do, do-dó-do-do, do . . .*

## Untitled prayer #6 (with very special guests Rush Lake and Picoides pubescens)

Pissing in cattails, one eye closed,
because sometimes I piss that way, I survey
half of all I can see. Being from here
makes me the product of a people
who use all the land they can
to grow soybeans and corn. I open the closed eye
because sometimes I piss that way, too,
see that being from here also means
I'm the product of strategically placed tree lines
and groves, of a people who suffer the wind.
If I could be a body of water
rather than one comprised mostly of it,
if I were skinned, de-boned, dispersed,
I would like to be a slough overgrown
with wild reeds, wild rice, bulrushes.
Prior to the beak-on-wood drumming
of a downy woodpecker
sessioning with a willow and grubs
I'd convinced myself I wanted to become
an ocean. Pissing, I've sunken an inch
at least, or two, into mud. Day before
Labor Day, before the side dishes and dips
I've promised to make are made
like yesterday isn't the day I'll
be granted any wish.

## Not everyone can carry the weight of the world goes the prayer


A photo of the last flowering
of the intermittently and night-blooming cactus
is what I keep in a cheap frame
next to the intermittently and night-blooming cactus itself
so that the photo is like a full-length mirror
designed by Charles Dickens' Ghost
of Christmas Past. I've given the cactus the ledge
that catches the best light, have set it
in a pot made of papier-mache, pot
that over-watering, overflowing
will disintegrate, making it a pot
that saves us, reminds of the perils
of too much, warns of drop offs, drowning,
swimming at our own risk. Trying on the cactus's
hat and shoes is like being a starlet
forced by management and circumstance
onto the last-chance comeback trail
where the understanding, hard-earned as a scar,
is that pinups emigrate
from bedroom walls to garages,
become Frankenstein monsters
in the minds of boys touching themselves,
blow-up dolls
with the pelvis and gams
of Lohan, torso of *Oops, I did it again*
Spears, hands of Barrymore, heart of Garland,
brain of Marilyn Monroe—
so beautifully hideous
that on the rare and heralded occasion
of blooming, the bloomer enjoys it least of anyone,
all the time thinking: anything I borrow from
tomorrow I owe.

## Who teaching whom: a prayer to be prayed next time you hear yourself say, "I've forgotten more than you'll ever know"

High schoolers
flood the neighborhood I live in
afternoons at three. They speak to each other
as if the distance from last class
to car provided an immunity
like the one you get from high dive
to splash. They're more than ready for summer
in the sense that summer is humid air imbued
with lilac incense lasting forever.
They're as suspicious
of men like me, who aren't at our jobs,
as birds are when a new feeder's fresh from the box,
full of foreign seed. I use my
*Mutual of Omaha's Wild Kingdom* overdub voice
to say to an audience of house plants and a cat
that while the high schoolers
may seem simply to be givers and getters
of a ride home, their interactions
are wildebeestean-crocodilean
at heart. Both givers and getters
swear in inventively vulgar spurts,
funnel past our houses so quickly
that rather than fertility
they leave dry gulches in their wakes.
For the plants, who have proven
easier to captivate than the cat, I rise
in defense of the givers' and getters'
use of mother-cock-sucking-hermaphrodite-horse-
fucker. They are trying to tell men like me
who have a midweek day off, or who work
from home, or who don't work at all,
gone DIY in garages, front yards,
on ladders, as fixated on our spheres of influence
as are raccoons who smell salmon
in a dumpster battened down
that while we may have a vision

of a pink and silver meal
we've forgotten
claws are the only tools we need.

## Prayer for those who feel trapped
## in a capitalist system

I earn money
so I can pay the daughter
who speaks English for her seamstress mom
ten dollars for a five-dollar patch
in the crotch of a pair of jeans
I've been fixing for twenty years.
The politics implied by the Levi's
are not my mother's. In the matter of underwear
mom counseled me to buy new yearly,
to throw out favorites if they're ragged,
worn thin, said I wouldn't want a rumor of shoddy briefs
to make it to the nurse's station, to become
*they are ill-mannered, know no better,*
*are probably poor.*
My mother's advice on underwear
as a correlative to reputation and namesake
is one example of a theme, a doctrine
from behind which a nation never emerges
in a cold war that lasts forever.
Like a chorus line of block letters lit at night,
all night, is the girl's family name.
She doesn't want to be the one responsible
for the pigeon shit
in the bowl of the family O.
I give her money. She gives me jeans.
She tries to give me money back.
I close my fist. With small, strong fingers
she tries to open it. She's not
the sun. My fist isn't a bud.

## If I could take what I know now, could put this brain into the body I had back then, is more or less how one of the oldest prayers in the world begins

I must have been pedaling at the speed of sound. How else
could I have come upon a baby-sitter,
crouched, administering to the baby-sat,
ass cheeks unfurling
from the low-cut waist of her jeans
like bread from a pan?
How else to come just as silently
upon the second faceless ass,
girl painting a dresser, bent like an L at the waist
to get as close as possible
to the handles, sweat pants fallen to the tuck
of her buttocks, held in the crease
like a bookmark?
How else could it have happened a third time
when a girl with a closet in a box
in the back seat of her car
didn't see me coming as she switched
from skirt to shorts behind the curtain
of a Volvo's door?
The Memory Department
in less than an hour
takes three underwearless asses
and however hairy, dimpled, and human they were
makes them as perfect as they'd be
airbrushed for a magazine.
The Bureau of Longing, which has never adhered
to the brain's moratorium on the dispensing
of leaflets of advice, notes that the promise of an ice cube
melting in the small of the back
is what would've made a younger me
who could pedal only 15 or 20 miles per hour,
25 on a good day, 30-plus with the wind,
stop to tell each of the girls "hello."
The Wisdom Desk, on behalf of the Embassy
Not of First But of Best Responses
as a gentle way of noting

I'm old enough to have sired them
sends a fax that says *Get some rest
for tomorrow. 186,000 miles per second's
a fucker to get into words.*

## Prayer for the journey: an accompaniment to "drive safe"

Sun eats fog leisurely. We're close to the river. It's morning. I point out the usual: pheasants, deer, turkey, afraid of it all, crouching in the ditch, tiptoeing at the edges of fields. I point out the opposite of the usual: hawk after hawk after hawk, who may be undercover police. "A bounty of hawks," I say to an imaginary traveling companion, a brunette modeled after an ex who insisted I name her tongue. A second imaginary companion modeled after a one-nighter who was more like an eighth-of-a-nighter, that eighth-of-a-night accountable ultimately for ending whatever I and the ex who made me call her tongue "killer" had—this blonde fling who wanted to do it in the front seat at the fairgrounds after the midway closed, and when I declined offered a menu of alternate places and ways to get off, most of which I also declined, thinking of how I'd hurt the ex not yet an ex—as she did then she does now, interceding from the back seat with "a fruit of hawks." It takes four minutes and ten seconds of hard thinking disguised as singing along to Madonna's "Crazy for You" before I can say of a hawk perched on mile marker 141, "It reminds me of a catalog model, the feathers like a pressed shirt and tailored suit, like it belongs in an ad." The ex, who is riding shotgun, who has had the cute vestigial skin tag she always swore she'd lance off lasered off, throws in with "an occurrence of hawks," which I almost don't hear wishing I could draw the skin tag back in, that a bloody scalpel had remained the hurdle she couldn't leap. The fling who had me more than I ever had her in those 75 minutes that have stretched into years, whose cigarette and sandpaper Demi Moore circa *St. Elmo's Fire* voice is as compelling and dangerous as the razor knives knife swallowers ask a member of the audience to touch, says, "a confluence of hawks." A third imaginary traveling companion, a redhead who in the aftermath of what happened with the fling and the ex dressed *I love you* in the late-80s slang version of *No strings attached*, joins in, joins us, and says, "a gathering of hawks." I point to a hawk on a wooden post, hawk that appears to be guarding a field of wheat, say "It reminds me of a political underdog, a long shot on election night memorizing two speeches as the results trickle in." As earnest and misunderstood and over-taught as a tour guide, I say that the highway we're driving follows more or less the overlap where the Mississippi and Central Flyways merge. The assembled imaginaries know me well enough to expect that in less than 24 hours I will look up and report that the two official names for a group of hawks are "kettle" and "cast." I should but do not know whether hawks migrate or whether these have simply taken advantage of the other birds' instincts to follow a path. The redhead, who has yet to move on, chimes in with, "an opportunity of hawks." Turns out an eighth of a night when I recalculate to include months-later skinnydipping is selling the blonde fling short. I acknowledge an eighth of a night plus, and she says, "A feed of hawks." I say, "If we're anything like the migratory birds, we'll winter as least as intimately as guests in adjoining rooms." Near Topeka we see what ends up being the last hawk of the day drenched in pink and orange, the sun a blooming coal. But people don't remember coals. People remember food. At a gas stop in Oklahoma I leave the imaginaries, except for Hegel, in the car. The clerk taking my money for a chocolate bar asks her companion clerk in the middle of my transaction if she noticed the hawks coming through. Waiting for Hegel, perched like a parrot on my shoulder, to reveal the self-evident, I say, "The last one I saw looked like the bud of a flag, where a brand new and better country, with an amazing constitution, available in PDF, wished it could begin." I fill the silence that follows, say, "We should spend every dollar we have translating the cease fire that the birds agree to in the south." Hegel says he'll meet me in the car. Dar (if her name tag is really hers) doesn't touch my hand when she gives me my change, universal way of asking, Mister, what planet are you from?

## Prayer that you, too, will receive such a gift when next you visit Eatonville, Florida

I went looking for Zora Neale Hurston
for light in the canopy of an old oak
something I could reasonably say
the way it drips
from pools on leaves
had inspired a page I've read
and what I found that said
*this is what you've been looking for*
was an old woman
skin as black as the black
inside a cave
black a little closer
to the wet-heat at the center of the earth
the porch this woman rocked on
had gone so far downhill
to seed
the wood so gray and smooth I bet
it was petrified
she stood
took a broom in her hands
herded the debris the afternoon storms
leave like a deposit at the bank
as if she owned
not only the weather
but the sky
and outer space
and the two knobs bulging
from her back
seemed to me were the nubs of wings
her humming grew to singing
to Hallelujah
to a red tongued and white toothed
boogie-woogie
she hiked up her dress
kicked off her shoes
lifted a bare foot in judgment
aimed it at my heart

intending to rip through bone
clench blood with her toes
I snapped a kind of photo
in my head
with my built-in fear cam
to be carried
prominently in my head-as-wallet
which that day I opened up and emptied
leaving all the mindmoney I had
on the sidewalk
understanding
my gooseflesh
which I had thought was saying
*run* wasn't
no, each tiny lump of me
was rising up as well as it could
in thanks.

## Ten ways of praying to the shadow (count 'em)

When the neighbor kids
play ball in the yard
I make a note. *Build a fence.*
*Protect the ferns.*
My shadow appears
like a mildly chiding parishioner
armed with the old responsorial psalm
about walking a mile in the moccasins,
heels, cleats of another.
Next time I'm hungry
I'll deny the body a meal, making it the scapegoat
for keeping things out.
Shadow, my work,
the dance of these hands,
collision and flutter
like sparrows mating midair,
puppet show I call, "Carpal Tunnel:
How it Electrifies the Wrists," what
I do for a wage is
not so far removed
from begging.
A cloud the color of iron
that can't or won't rain
is the shadow I make in the sky.
If the boys with the plastic bat
and ball looked in they'd see
me knee to wood, face of need on a craning neck,
shadow of a man in a Moses pose
wearing a white tee
and blue jeans, supplicant
before a burning bush
that isn't there.
I love watching shadows mime
the showing of tolerance
to customers returning merchandise
the store has never sold.
Shadow, I position my body at an angle to the light,
yield your twelve-foot rendition

of deaf-mute me.
Shadow, do the ignorances
however blissful
of one-dimensionality
make you envy my larynx
and singing?
I can make you do the robot
winding down, losing charge slowly,
head staring at empty hands
in order to show you *crestfallen*,
how I feel since the whiskey glass
that survived a drop at the party last night
after previously surviving
the Korean War, Sputnik, Integration, Nixon
in my grandfather's cupboard, in his grip—
it broke today as I was drying it
with a thin white cloth.
It takes everything I've got
to keep from screaming
when I stub my toe
looking for the broom,
for the dustpan it divorced. I limp
a few steps, like I'm dragging a polio leg,
give in, lean against a wall. Below me,
Shadow, you've assumed the position
one assumes for frisking. I forget
why I've come to where I am,
try to walk it off
like the conjoined twin
who didn't die in the surgery
to separate.

## Pray that we always fight the good fight (Prince Namor's lullaby)

My landlord shaves every day
will never believe the truth
a strong wind broke my window
middle of summer, gorgeous afternoon
the way Thor's hammer
dropped from Asgard
while the God of Thunder daydreams
or gets lucky
makes a tsunami
of a glassy bay (or in winter
splinters the surface
of a frozen lake)
I'll have to make up a lie
say drunks, vandals, revolutionaries
threw a bottle during the night, that
the neighbor kid hit a grand slam homerun
then ditched, lie
or fix it myself with duct tape, less
man than fish.

## Prayer to the shape-shifting god, now goddess of motion, who more often than not appears to us in the form of a stone

The voice on the radio
says the temperature today will dip
gradually below thirty, twenty, fifteen,
tonight below ten.
The voice sounds like it's molting,
like essential parts of wings
are being dropped from it.
I breathe in deep, am a bag of gas
with the frivolous ability to envision the radio man
as a bird. I breathe out
until I can't breathe out anymore,
am a bag
for tires and shoes and news
to leave their marks upon.
In the passenger's seat, what I've breathed out
congeals. I say, *Breath in the shape of a Buddha,*
*soak into things,*
face what I've said, how I've said it,
second congealing, two Buddhas wrestling,
descent into Sumo.
Like a deer
paralyzed by a Subaru's headlights,
I hold my next breath in.
I've been issued boards, nails, a hammer,
caulk, and drywall,
am expected to build.
My father
said warm up the engine
before you shift into drive.
I'd be any of the stitches in a hair shirt
if you'd wear it.
Minutes ago I was reading
from my dead aunt's copy of *Webster's*
*Fifth Collegiate Dictionary*, flipping
through the "New Words" addition of 1941.
May as well have been looking at old light

through a telescope, discovering
prior to my birth was a time
when I couldn't look up *fiberglass,*
*racism, blitzkrieg, jam session,*
or *station wagon,*
when if I looked up *stop*
I wouldn't find a definition
of its photographic sense,
sadder time
when *stop* didn't resemble me in the slightest,
who if I were named now
would be called
he who has no good reason
to move the car,
being weighed down as he is
by a sense of *stop* that means
the aperture of a lens.

## Passing (nee praising) the laundromat (Grand and 36th) my head as unbloodied as it is unbowed

A pair of brown socks

held above the basket
by a short brown woman

to the window
to see if they match

aren't socks
but the eyes of my grandmother.

You can see (only) so much
from the saddle of a bike.

A pair of blue socks
held up next are crying.

I'll never know for whom, nor why, nor which ghost's
eyes produce cerulean tears.

I wave at the socks:
another example of how the dead and I
envy each other.

The short brown woman
is a butterfly

unable to fly. I ride away,
her only wing.

# ACKNOWLEDGMENTS

Versions* of these poems appeared in: *DIAGRAM*, "Prayer for those flying solo on jet planes ascending and descending through turbulence who are reminded of the ghost on a bicycle ghost-riding stairs"; *Sonora Review*, "Black wool as the answer to everything, the antidote for, the synonym of, in medias res, black wool is love—" (finalist in the Sonora Review Poetry Contest); *Willow Springs*, "A conversation that sounds like me praying to the ghost of James Wright as if he were here in the passenger seat and what I say might yet become an annotation to 'A Blessing'"; *The Los Angeles Review*, "Pray that it were otherwise, but the hard work of life isn't in the tapping of the true thought, but in the building of a pipeline to deliver the goods"; *The World According to Goldfish, Vols. I & II* (Goldfish Press Anthologies), "Prayer for old fish, hail to their beards of monofilament," "The moon tonight inspires not only wonder and tides but also this deathbedish prayer," "Prayer to bestow a blessing on the city," "Prayer to encourage the seizing of the day"; *Tule Review*, "If I could take what I know now, could put this brain into the body I had back then, is more or less how one of the oldest prayers in the world begins"; *Poetry Daily*, "The human palimpsest's prayer."

Versions* of the following poems appear in the chapbook *The Book of Modern Prayer* (Palimpsest Press 2010): "Livin' on a prayer," "Prayer to that which accepts me in sacrifice," "Crimes of the heart: a prayer to the patron saint of that, on the lam for life," "Prayer like the punch line that isn't funny to the joke that begins, 'So this pagan and this transubstantiator walk into a bar'," "Psalm for the working class in a totalitarian regime doing double duty as a prayer for the same class opiated by dreams of wealth in a capitalistic one," "The human palimpsest's prayer," "The moon tonight inspires not only wonder and tides but also this deathbedish prayer," "Prayer for my oldest teachers," "Prayer for ferrying," "Prayer to bestow a blessing on the city," "Drinking feels like praying when done across the street from a beach where emergency response crews have been conducting a lake search for over an hour," "Walking is a kind of prayer when done on new snow after midnight," "Shopping during the afternoon rush, not buying items on my list if the artery in which the thing is found is clogged with humanity, composing as I nod hello this prayer for intestinal fortitude," "From a parking lot, in an unfamiliar part of town, eating take-out sushi, listening to talk radio during a midday break, day of mandatory training, comes this prayer of gratitude for all of the above," "Untitled prayer #6 (with very special guests Rush Lake and Picoides pubescens)," "Prayer for those who feel trapped in a capitalist system," "Prayer for the journey: an accompaniment to 'drive safe'," "Ten ways of praying to the shadow (count 'em)," "Prayer to the shape-shifting god, now goddess of motion, who more often than not appears to us in the form of a stone," "Waiting for fireworks: an Independence Day prayer," "Passing (nee praising) the laundromat (Grand and 36th) my head as unbloodied as it is unbowed."

* The word "versions" always reminds me of the note on the back of The Jam's double LP *Snap!*. In red letters in a margins-justified block of type it says "'FUNERAL PYRE' WAS REMIXED IN AUGUST 1983 AS NOBODY WAS COMPLETELY HAPPY WITH THE ORIGINAL MIX. IT WAS DECIDED TO USE THE DEMO VERSION OF 'THAT'S ENTERTAINMENT' ON THIS L.P. ALTHOUGH TECHNICALLY NOT AS GOOD AS THE LATER VERSION RECORDED FOR 'SOUND EFFECTS,' THE DEMO HAS A CERTAIN QUALITY THAT WAS NEVER CAPTURED AGAIN." *mm*

# NOTES

*Page 28*    The cop quotations come from the *SF Gate/San Francisco Chronicle* article "Cracking the Code of Silence" by Stephanie Salter (Sunday, March 9, 2003).

*Page 61*    Miss Noi is a character in the story "Fairy Tale," from Robert Olen Butler's *A Good Scent from a Strange Mountain*.

# THANK YOUs

Thanks to the editors and staffs of the journals on the opposite page. Big thanks, too, to the one publisher on the opposite page, Dawn Kresen of Palimpsest Press.

Thank you Monica Fambrough, and thank you Denny Schmickle.

Thanks to the English Department at Briar Cliff College (sic), without the influence of which I was well on my way to a career as an engineer or a lawyer. Thanks to the creative writing faculty at Mankato State University (sic), who brought me up to speed. As well, thanks to faculty and staff at the Squaw Valley Community of Writers. Risk, etc., had been missing elements.

Thanks to the readers, my poet-and-writer-friends, whose advice, direct and otherwise, made these poems and this book what it is: Kris Bigalk, Todd Boss, Alicia Conroy, Layla Dowlatshahi, Kassie Duthie, Marguerite Harrold, Liberty Heise, Kelli Johnson, Tom Maltman, Theresa McCourt, Eric Mein, John Reimringer, Lynette Reini-Grandell, Charlotte Sullivan, and Liz Weir.

Thank you, for buying this.

Dobby Gibson, MC Hyland, Brad Liening, Paisley Rekdal, Rick Robbins, Wesley Stace, and Matt Ryan: effusive and sentimental thanks.

I would be remiss without a shout out to Wednesday, Zooey, and the late Wellstone, who endured more out-loud iterations of the these poems than is humanly tolerable. So it's good that they're not. Humans.

Thanks to my family. Stay gold.

And from the halls of 709 S. Second Street to the shores of So. Mpls, via Nebraska, a word I don't know that means "the biggest 'thank you' of them all" is reserved for Angie. That word to the power of infinity.

# ABOUT THE AUTHOR

Matt Mauch (www.mauchmauch.com) grew up in small Midwestern towns between the Missouri and Mississippi rivers, in the snow and wind-chill belt, where he worked as a foreman on a corn de-tasseling crew, as a women's shoes salesman, and in a Goodyear shop where he changed oil in everything from cars to milk trucks, mounting and dismounting (and sometimes patching) semi truck tires on a daily basis. He is the author of the chapbook *The Book of Modern Prayer* (Palimpsest Press, 2010). His poems have recently appeared in *Salt Hill*, *NOÖ Journal*, *H_NGM_N*, *DIAGRAM*, *Willow Springs*, *Tule Review*, *The Los Angeles Review*, and *Sonora Review*. The editor of *Poetry City, USA, Vol. 1* (Lowbrow Press, 2011), Mauch teaches writing and literature in the AFA program at Normandale Community College, and also coordinates the reading series there. He lives in Minneapolis.

*[author photo by Sydnee Bickett]*

Made in the USA
Charleston, SC
30 October 2011